Copyright © 2023 Jennifer Jones
All copyright laws and rights reserved. Published in the U.S.A.
For more information, email info@ninjalifehacks.tv
Paperback ISBN: 978-1-63731-849-2 Hardcover ISBN: 978-1-63731-851-5
eBook ISBN: 978-1-63731-850-8

Find the Sharpeners on Strike lesson plans at ninjalifehacks.tv

In every school classroom,
beside the shelf that holds the books,
we sit on top of a table,
if you only take a look.

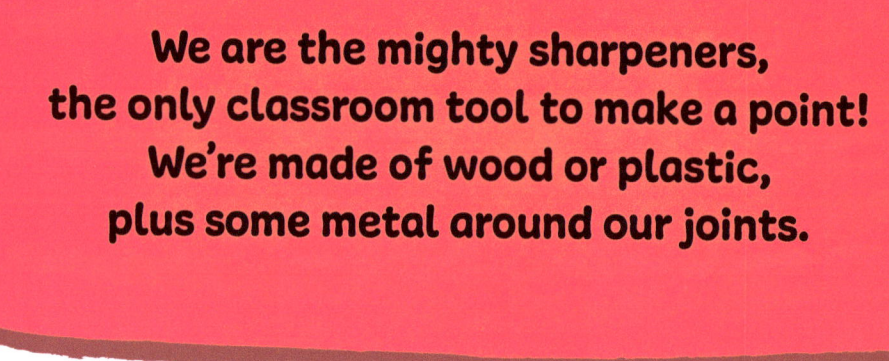

We proudly take dull pencils
and help students grind them to be of use.
Without us, pencils would not write.
Students would have no idea what to do.

Some of us are electric.
We do the work without turning a wheel
which is likely why students started treating us
without any regard for how we feel.

Officially, we're known as "Sharpeners."
We know it's a long, serious word.
Some students struggle to call us by the right name
which, to us, seems kind of absurd.

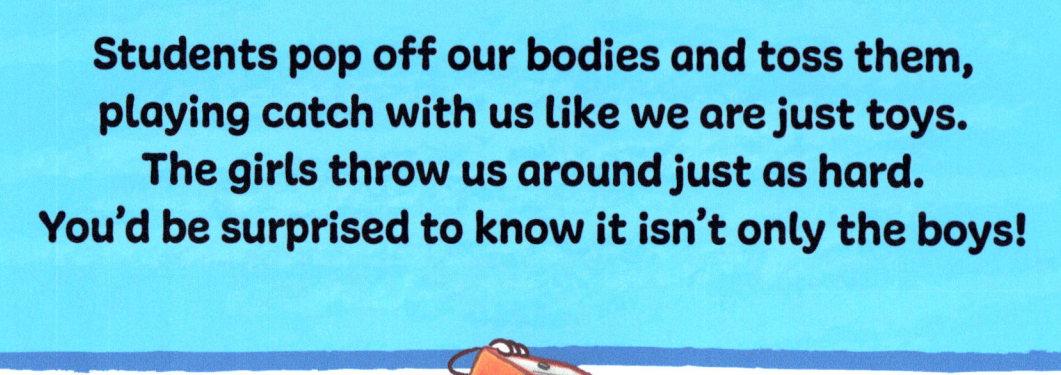

Students pop off our bodies and toss them,
playing catch with us like we are just toys.
The girls throw us around just as hard.
You'd be surprised to know it isn't only the boys!

Sometimes, when they dump out shavings,
they drop us in the trash too.
The teacher tells them to pick us up,
but they only do what they want to do.

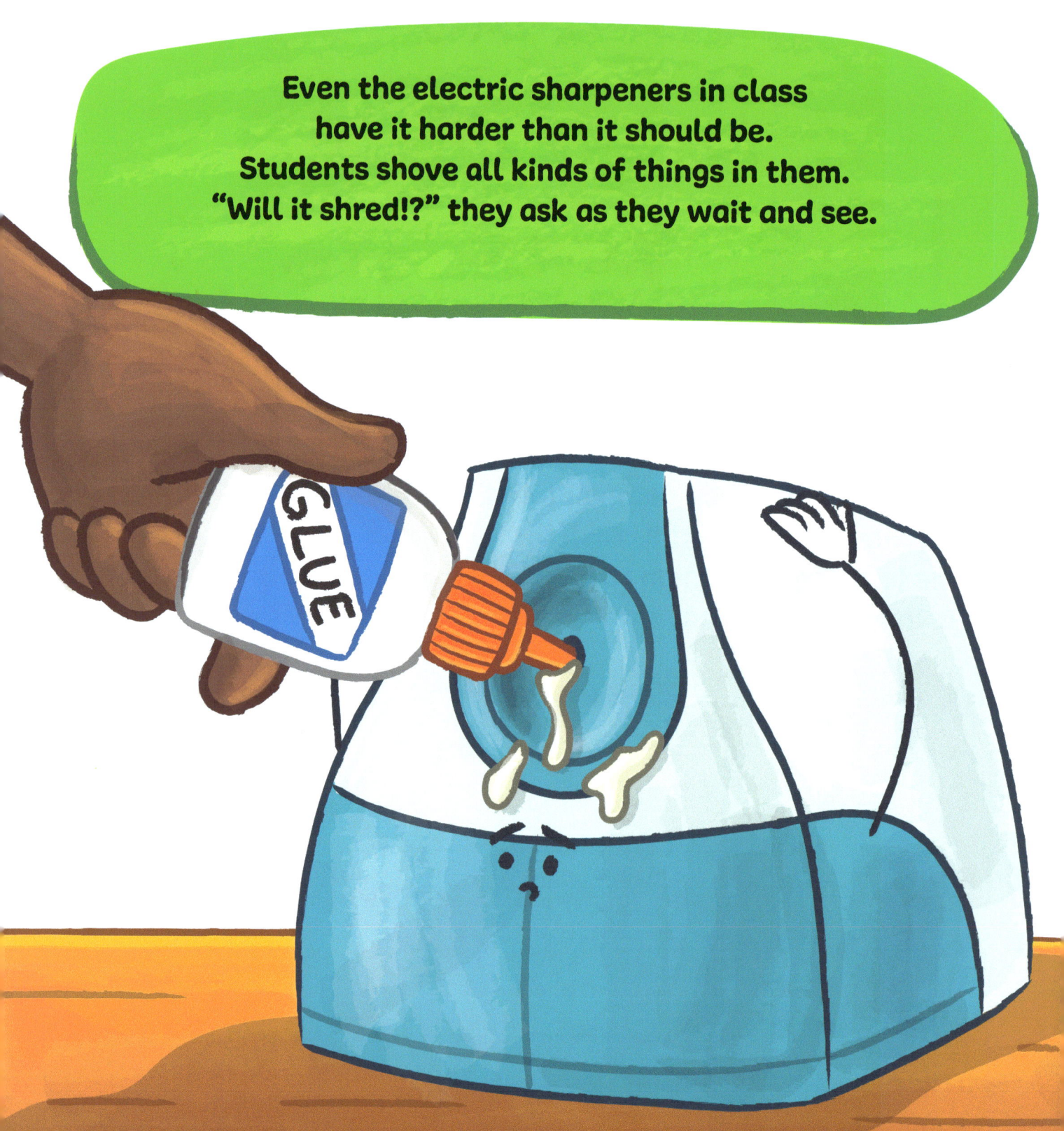

They put pencils in backwards first.
Let the erasers get stuck in our gears.
Do you know the sound shredding metal makes?
It's worse than all of your fears!

As soon as class was dismissed,
and the students scurried out of the room,
we called over paper and pencils,
from the blue bin next to the broom.

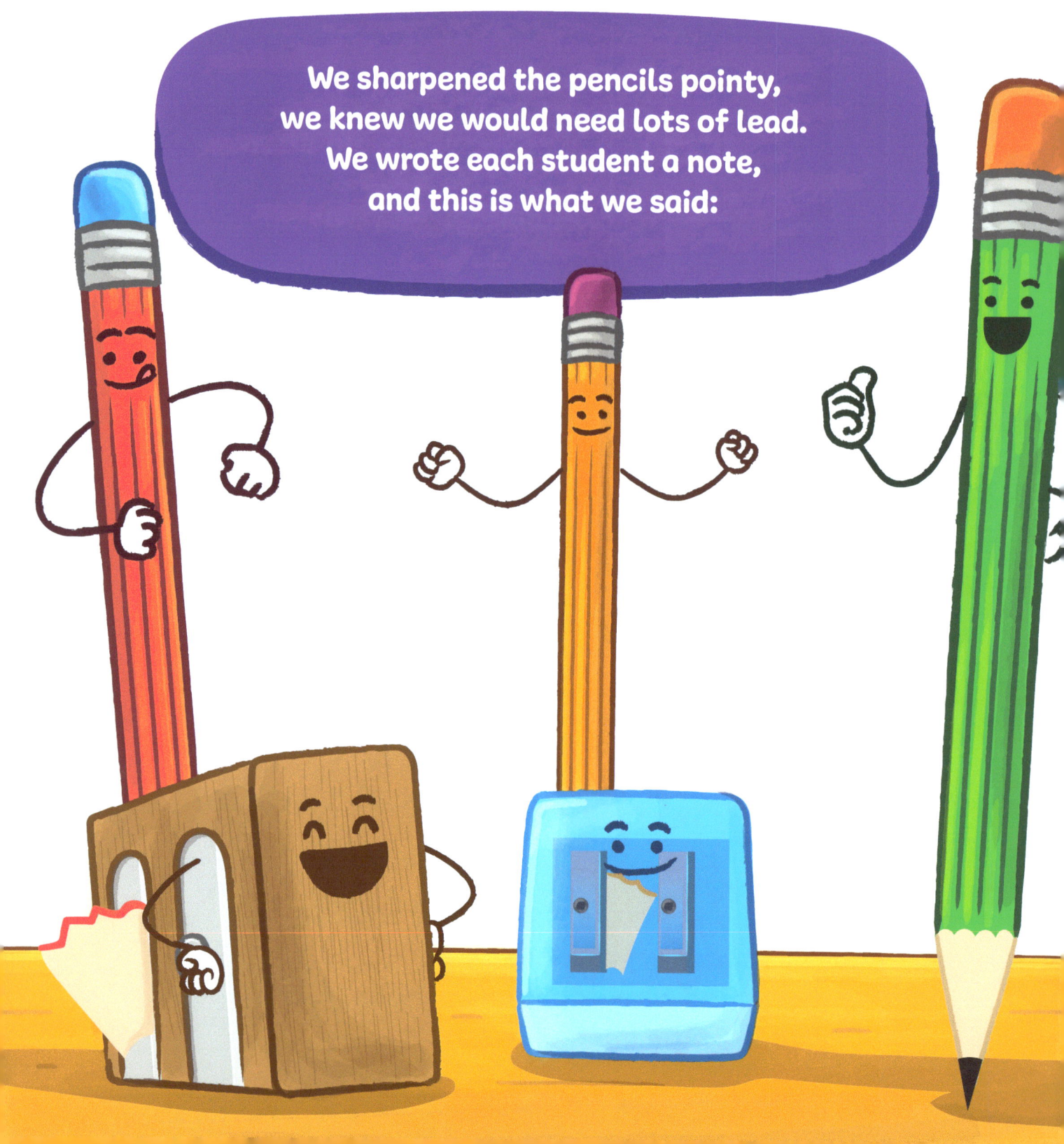

Dear Student,

We're so sad about your actions.

You treat us however you like.

Until you learn kindess and respect,

we, the sharpeners, are going on strike!

The students wrote back to our letter and apologized for treating us the way that they did.

Please come back, we can be better. We're sorry, it's our fault you hid!

www.ingramcontent.com/pod-product-compliance
Lightning Source LLC
Chambersburg PA
CBHW041714160426
43209CB00018B/1830